Ben is a big bug.
Ben has a mud hut.

Ben is sad.
His mud hut got wet.
It has a lot of wet mud.
Ben can not get in it.

Ben had to get a hut.
It is hot in the sun.

Ben met a man.
The man had a hat.

Ben ran up to the hat.
It was a big hat.

Ben was hot.
It was a big job to tug
on the hat.

Ben can not get in
the hat.
Ben got a pin and cut
the hat.

The hat has a big rip
in it.
Ben got in and sat.
The big hat is his hut.
It is not hot in the hut.

Ben got a big nut and
set it in his hut.
The nut is his tub.
Ben got in his tub
and got wet.

Ben has a bed.
A big pod is his bed.
Ben got in his bed
and had a nap.

The man is hot.
The man ran to get
his hat.

Ben ran to the nut
and hid.
Ben is big, but a bug is
not as big as a man.

The man ran
to the hat.
The man got his hat,
but the hat had a rip
in it.

Ben ran and hid.
Ben is a sad bug.

The man got Ben and
set him on a tin can.
The man is not mad.
The tin can is not big,
but Ben can fit in it.

The tin can has a lid.
Ben got up on it.
It is fun to hop on it.
A tin can is not a
bad hut.